NoLex 11/12

Outlaws and Lawmen of the Wild West

BAT MASTERSON

Carl R. Green

≫ and ≪

William R. Sanford

ENSLOW PUBLISHERS, INC.

Bloy St. & Ramsey Ave.   P.O. Box 38
Box 777   Aldershot
Hillside, N.J. 07205   Hants GU12 6BP
U.S.A.   U.K.

Library of Congress Cataloging-in-Publication Data

Green, Carl R.
  Bat Masterson / Carl R. Green and William R. Sanford.
    p. cm. — (Outlaws and lawmen of the Wild West)
  Includes bibliographical references and index.
  Summary: Chronicles the life of the Western lawman Bat Masterson, who later
became a New York sports writer.
  ISBN 0-89490-362-4
  1. Masterson, Bat, 1853–1921—Juvenile literature. 2. Peace officers—West (U.S.)—
Biography—Juvenile literature. [1. Masterson, Bat, 1853–1921. 2. Peace officers.]
I. Sanford, William R. (William Reynolds), 1927– . II. Title. III. Series: Green, Carl
R. Outlaws and lawmen of the Wild West.
  F594.M33G74 1992
  978'.02'092—dc20
  [B]   91-29857
                                                           CIP
                                                            AC

Printed in the United States of America

10 9 8 7 6 5 4 3 2

Illustration Credits:
Amon Carter Museum, Fort Worth, Texas, p. 41; Denver Public Library, Western
History Department, pp. 6, 9, 13, 17, 20, 29, 34, 44; Carl R. Green and William R.
Sanford, p. 10; Kansas Sate Historical Society, Topeka, Kansas, pp. 19, 21, 22, 23, 27,
31, 37, 38, 40.

Cover Illustration:
Michael David Biegel

CONTENTS

AUTHORS' NOTE

This book tells the true story of a lawman named Bat Masterson. Bat was as well known in his lifetime as rock stars are now. His exploits appeared in newspapers, magazines, and dime novels. In more recent times Bat has been featured in films and on television. Some of the stories were made up, but many were true. The events described in this book all come from firsthand reports.

1
MAKE THE
FIRST SHOT COUNT

Bat Masterson won fame in the Wild West as a lawman and a gunslinger. He wore his lawman's badges with pride. Being called a gunslinger was another matter. To Bat, gunslingers were hoodlums who killed for fun. He used his guns to enforce the law or defend a friend.

A new deputy once asked Bat about guns. Bat said, "The main thing is shoot first and never miss. Never try to run a bluff with a six-gun. Many a man has been buried with his boots on because he foolishly tried to scare someone by reaching for his hardware. Always remember that a six-shooter is made to kill the other fellow with and for no other reason. So always have your gun loaded and ready. Never reach for it unless you are in dead earnest and intend to kill the other fellow."

Bat told the deputy not to aim at his foe's head.

Young Bat Masterson displays the cool, steady gaze of the gunfighter. A man must not draw his gun unless he intends to use it, he said. In his own lifetime, Bat followed that advice. He did not draw often, but he did not miss when he did.

"Never do that," he said. "If you have to stop a man with a gun, grab . . . your six-shooter with a death grip that won't let it wobble. Try to hit him just where the belt buckle would be. That's the broadest target from head to foot."

First a gunfighter must have the courage to draw his pistol, Bat went on. Second he must be able to shoot fast and straight. Most of all, Bat said, a man had to be cool and steady. If he did not make the first shot count, he might not have a second chance.

Legends say that Bat killed 20 or more men. In fact, the number was much closer to four. Bat Masterson somehow survived a violent age without becoming a violent man.

2
GROWING UP ON THE FRONTIER

Bartholomew Masterson was born in Canada in 1853. He was the second son of Thomas and Catherine Masterson. The boy disliked his name. When he was older he changed it to William Barclay Masterson. The family called him Bart at first, then Bat.

During the next eight years Catherine gave birth to five more children. After Ed and Bat came James, Nellie, Tom, George, and Emma. In 1861 the search for good land drew Thomas to upstate New York. From there he moved his family to Illinois. Somewhere out on the frontier, Thomas dreamed, was the perfect farm.

Young Bat was a lively, active boy. He was often in trouble for playing pranks. School was not the place Bat liked best. When the teacher was not looking, he slipped out of school to go hunting. Bat's gun was an old muzzle-loading rifle that he talked his father into buying. He soon became a crack shot.

In 1871 Thomas found what he was looking for in Sedgwick County, Kansas. He bought 80 acres of rich farmland. The land was close to what later became the rip-roaring cowtown of Wichita. Bat and Ed helped their father plow his fields that summer. Then they left home to find work and adventure.

At first the boys hired out as buffalo skinners. Then, in 1872, they found work with Ray Ritter. Their job was to level the railroad right-of-way. Behind them crews laid the tracks for the Atchison, Topeka, & Santa Fe Railroad. As soon as the work was done Ritter took off

Thomas and Catherine Masterson lived in this farmhouse near Sedgwick, Kansas. Here, they are about to drive their buggy to town. Bat was their second son. He left home with his older brother Ed after the family homesteaded this land.

Bat Masterson was born in Canada, but won enduring fame as a lawman in the American West.

without paying them. Bat and Ed were left in Dodge City, Kansas with no money.

To earn a living the brothers joined a group of buffalo hunters. The men sold the meat to railroad workers in Dodge City. The hides were dried and shipped east. In those days buffalo were easy to find in Kansas. When the hunters found a herd they rode in close and killed 30 or 40 animals at a time. Then they removed the hides and cut out the best pieces of meat. The bodies were left to rot.

Buffalo hunting was hard work. Ed and Bat put in seven long days a week. When the herds moved south for the winter the hunters followed. Cold weather made the job even harder. If the men did not work swiftly, the dead buffalo froze before they could be skinned.

In the spring of 1873 Bat proved he could use a gun. A friend told him that Ray Ritter was on the Dodge City train. Bat met the train and marched Ritter off it at gunpoint. Pay me my money, Bat warned, or you won't get back on that train alive. Ritter looked into the hard

As a young man, Bat made his living as a buffalo hunter. Hunters lived off the land, shooting game for food and enduring bad weather. In order to survive, Bat learned to work hard and to shoot straight.

blue-gray eyes and believed the threat. He counted out $300 and handed the money to Bat.

By 1874 the Kansas buffalo herds were thinning out. Hunters coming through Dodge said the animals were plentiful in Texas. There was one catch. The Medicine Lodge Treaty of 1867 reserved the area to Indian hunters. That did not bother Bat and his friends. Their feelings were typical of the times. Where Indians could hunt buffalo, they said, white men should be able to do the same.

Fifty men and 30 wagons left Dodge City in March 1874. Twenty-year-old Bat was the youngest hunter in the group. The wagon train headed for a spot in the Texas Panhandle called Adobe Walls. There the men found a saloon built of sod, a stable, a blacksmith shop, and a trading post. The little settlement became their base.

One morning in May, Bat heard a welcome noise. The distant bellow of the buffalo sounded like trains rumbling over a wooden bridge. Soon the great herds swept across the plains. Armed with .50-caliber rifles, the men began the killing. Each day they rode out, shot buffalo, and skinned them. The hides were piled into wagons to be carried back to Adobe Walls.

The local tribes saw the slaughter and feared the white men would destroy the herds. War leaders met and agreed to drive the white hunters from the prairie. A Comanche chief named Quanah Parker was chosen to lead the attack. A medicine man smeared the braves

Quanah Parker led the attack on the buffalo hunters at Adobe Walls.
Quanah's father was a Comanche chief and his mother was white. His
warriors were hurled back by the firepower of the Adobe Walls defenders.

with magic war paint. He told them the paint would protect them from the white men's bullets.

Word reached Adobe Walls that the Comanches were on the warpath. A few men fled, but Bat and most of the hunters stayed. Early in the morning of June 27 the men awoke to a sharp cracking noise. It sounded as though the saloon's roof was about to fall in. Men climbed to the roof and removed strips of sod to lighten the weight. As dawn broke one of the workers spotted a dust cloud raised by war ponies. His warning came just in time.

Hundreds of warriors attacked Adobe Walls. Thirty-eight men and one woman loaded their rifles and waited inside the settlement. The Comanches killed four hunters caught in the open. The assault on the thick-walled buildings was another matter. The magic war paint could not stop .50-caliber slugs. Despite their losses the Comanches pressed the attack. A few came close enough to fire through slits in the walls.

At last Chief Quanah pulled his men back. Unable to kill the hunters, he drove off all their horses. Then he sent roving bands of warriors to keep a loose watch on the white men. With luck Quanah might have starved the hunters out. But men on horseback slipped into Adobe Walls from an outlying camp. Using the new horses Bat and some friends set out to bring help.

The rescue party made it to Dodge City. When they arrived they were cheered as heroes. They also learned that the risky trip was not needed. A relief party was already on its way to Adobe Walls.

The Red River War with the Plains Indians broke out that same year. The fighting cut short the buffalo hunting season. In need of a job, Bat joined the U.S. Army. He became a scout for a unit of cavalry which was training to ride against the tribes. Scouts were paid $75 a month for serving as the Army's eyes and ears.

Helped by cold weather the soldiers drove the Plains Indians back to their reservations. Bat stayed on in Sweetwater, Texas, when the fighting ended. He was looking for fun, but he almost died in a gunfight instead.

DODGE CITY LAWMAN

Bat never forgot the night of January 24, 1876. The evening started in a Sweetwater saloon. Bat was dancing there with Molly Brennan. A soldier named Melvin King walked in and saw them. King was a jealous man who wanted Molly for himself. He pulled his gun without warning and fired at Bat. The bullet ripped through Molly's stomach and shattered Bat's hip. As Bat fell he pulled his own gun. His shot slammed into King's chest, killing him. Molly was already dead.

King's friends moved in to kill Bat. A gambler named Ben Thompson stopped them. He said that shooting a wounded man was unfair. Then he pulled his six-guns and told the cowboys to stand back. They obeyed, not wanting to take on the deadeye gambler. Bat's friends carried him to an Army doctor. The doctor did his best, but Bat's hip did not mend fully. From that time on he walked with the aid of a cane.

When Bat was well enough to ride he returned to Dodge City. His buffalo-hunting friend Wyatt Earp was now chief deputy marshal there. Bat and his brother Jim hired on as deputies. Wyatt knew that both men could handle themselves in a fight. The town paid Bat $75 a month. He also earned a share of the fines that the lawmen collected.

Dodge City was two towns in one. North of the railroad tracks lay the hotels and stores. South of the tracks were dance halls, honky-tonk saloons, and gambling halls. The town served as a railhead for the cattle

Englishman Ben Thompson was a western gambler and gunman. In later years, Bat claimed that no one could equal Ben in a "life and death struggle." The night Bat traded shots with Melvin King, Ben saved his life. The gambler held King's friends back long enough for Bat to be carried to safety.

driven north from Texas each year. By the time the cowboys reached Dodge, they were ready to cut loose. To keep the peace the town's lawmen did not allow them to wear guns north of the tracks.

Cane in hand, Bat patrolled the streets of Dodge. Cowboys who did not know him said he looked as though he should have been directing funerals. Bat wore a black suit, a white shirt, and a string tie. Instead of a cowboy hat he wore a derby. At five feet, nine inches he was not a tall man. Even so, the cowboys soon learned to respect him. As his friend Billy Dixon said, "He was a chunk of steel. Anything that struck him in those days always drew [sparks]."

Bat carried two pistols when he was on duty. But he seldom used them. More often he knocked drunken cowboys senseless with his cane. If he could keep the peace without making an arrest, he did so. Bat often tossed drunks into a horse trough or rain barrel. After he fished the men out he urged them to go sleep it off.

Dodge City was located in Ford County, Kansas. In November 1877 Bat ran for county sheriff. He won the job by only three votes. The huge county covered almost a thousand square miles. In the weeks that followed Bat crisscrossed the region in pursuit of train robbers. Blessed with luck and good sense, he caught the crooks and put them in jail.

Bat's easygoing brother Ed was having his own success in Dodge City. As a deputy marshal he impressed

Thanks to the Santa Fe railway, Dodge City was a busy cowtown in 1878. Front Street's stores and saloons looked peaceful during the day. At night, fresh from the cattle drives, fun-loving cowboys rode into town to drink and gamble. Keeping the peace when the cowboys were in town was a big job for a lawman.

the town with his cool courage. Ed often used Bat's method of cracking drunks over the head. Called to break up a fight one night, he did not hit one drunk hard enough. The man shook off the blow, turned his gun on Ed, and shot him. Luckily the wound was not fatal. When Ed returned to duty he was given the job of town marshal.

Ed's luck soon changed. He got into a fight one night with another drunk. When Ed tried to arrest the cowboy, the man's gun went off. The bullet blew a hole clear through Ed's stomach. Despite the pain Ed drew his own gun and killed the cowboy. Then he walked 200 yards to a saloon and fainted. He died an hour later in Bat's arms. "This will about kill his ma," Bat mourned. "She'll never forgive me for letting Ed get killed."

Ed Masterson was Bat's easygoing older brother. He was also a fine Dodge City lawman in his own right. His luck ran out in 1878 when he tried to disarm a drunken cowboy. The gun went off blowing a hole through Ed's stomach.

Legends say that Bat avenged Ed's death by shooting the four men who were with Ed's killer. That is a dramatic story. The truth is less bloody. After Ed died Bat simply arrested the four cowboys. Then Bat gave Ed a proper funeral at the Fort Dodge cemetery. He refused to bury his brother in Dodge City's Boot Hill. That was where all the good-for-nothing gunmen were buried.

A sheriff's life in the Old West was seldom dull. In 1878 George Hoyt came to Dodge City looking for a good time. Hoyt's idea of fun was to wildly fire his rifle as he rode through town. Bat, off duty at the time, was dealing cards in a music hall. He dropped to the floor as bullets whizzed past. When the firing stopped Bat and

Fannie Garretson starred at Ben Springer's Comique in Dodge City. She left town, however, in fear for her life. One night she and another performer, Dora Hand, slept in Mayor Kelley's house. That was the night Jim Kennedy picked to take a shot at the mayor. He fired into the house, barely missing Fannie and killing Dora. Bat led the posse that captured the killer.

Wyatt Earp chased the cowboy. Wyatt shot Hoyt out of his saddle.

Some time later Clay Allison came to town to avenge his friend's death. Legend says that Bat "hid in a hole" when Clay rode in that day. That story was passed around by men who did not like Bat. In fact, he was out of town at the time. Clay did have a run-in with Wyatt. Their brief fight ended without gunplay.

Bat returned to town in time to arrest some Indian raiders. Chief Dull Knife had led a band of Cheyenne off their reservation. The Indians burned ranches and killed some farmers. The Army drove the raiders away, but Kansans wanted revenge. Bat was sent to Fort Leavenworth to pick up seven Indian prisoners. He brought them back to Dodge in chains. A trial was held, but the case was dismissed for lack of evidence.

As sheriff of Ford County, Bat was the chief lawman for a huge territory. When he incurred extra costs, he billed the county for his expenses. This check for $35 was issued in January of 1879. Some checks were much larger. Bat once billed the county $4,000—the cost of keeping seven prisoners for five months.

The record shows that Bat was a good sheriff. A strong lawman makes enemies, however. When election time drew near in 1879 his enemies spread rumors that he was a crook. Bat refused to defend himself. He thought his friends would stand up for him. Perhaps they did, but too many people believed the rumors. Bat lost the election. When January came he was out of a job.

Once as sheriff, Bat was sent to pick up these seven Cheyenne prisoners. The Indians had been part of a raiding party led by Chief Dull Knife. Here, with hands bound by shackles, they wait for trial. George Reynolds, seated in the first row, served as their interpreter.

4
FROM LEADVILLE TO TOMBSTONE

Bat Masterson was only 26 when he left Dodge City. For eight years he had worked as a buffalo hunter, Army scout, and lawman. Along the way he had also gained fame as a gambler. In those days honest gamblers were treated with respect. Bat played a cool, heady game of cards—and often won.

In 1880 Bat headed for the silver mining town of Leadville, Colorado. He knew Leadville well, for he had taken part in the Royal Gorge War in 1879. This strange war had been fought between two railroad companies. One company was the Denver & Rio Grande railroad. The other was the Atchison, Topeka, & Santa Fe. Both railroads wanted to lay track into Leadville. Clearly, the only route lay through the Royal Gorge of the Arkansas River. The railroad that controlled the gorge, therefore, would gain the right to haul Leadville's silver ore.

The war was fought on two levels. On one level lawyers argued the case in the courts. Out in the Royal Gorge, on another level, small armies built stone forts. Hired gunmen prepared to battle for control of the gorge. In March of 1879 the Santa Fe hired Bat to guard its stations and work crews. Bat took a posse of 33 men to the mouth of the gorge at Canon City. The Rio Grande's gunmen were there ahead of him. Patient as always Bat waited to see what the courts would do. When the Rio Grande railroad won its case, he took his men back to Dodge.

A few weeks later Bat was back with more hired guns. The conflict now centered on the town of Pueblo. Bat turned the railroad station and roundhouse into forts. His men were armed with shotguns, rifles, pistols, and a rapid-fire Gatling gun. In Denver, the Rio Grande men had already killed two Santa Fe men. Now they were ready to drive Bat's force out of Pueblo.

The Rio Grande "army" was led by R. F. Weitbrec, the line's treasurer. After Weitbrec's men captured the railway station they moved against the roundhouse. General Palmer, the Rio Grande's president, wanted to attack. Weitbrec had other ideas. Under cover of a white flag he set up a talk with Bat. An hour later Bat surrendered the roundhouse without firing a shot.

Some of Bat's critics claimed that Weitbrec paid him $10,000 to give up. It is true that Bat was fond of money. A more likely story is that Weitbrec showed Bat a legal paper. The court order gave control of the Santa Fe station to the Rio Grande railroad. Besides, Weitbrec must have added, the other stations on the line were already in his hands. More bloodshed would have been foolish.

When Bat returned to Colorado in 1880 the Royal Gorge War was over. The Denver & Rio Grande had agreed not to build lines to St. Louis or El Paso. For its part the Santa Fe promised not to build a line to Leadville. Now Bat was free to spend his time at the card tables. Leadville was a gambler's paradise. In Dodge the betting limit was $25 a card. In Leadville there was no betting limit. Men bet thousands of dollars on the turn of a single card.

Bat found that he did not enjoy Colorado's cold, snowy winters. Early in 1881 he went back to Kansas. He was playing poker in Kansas City when he received a telegram from Tombstone, Arizona. Wyatt Earp needed his help.

Bat knew that Wyatt was the U.S. Marshal for the wild mining town. Wyatt did not ask Bat to serve as his deputy. He needed someone to help Luke Short keep the peace in his Oriental Saloon. The other saloon owners were jealous of the Oriental's success. Some of them were hiring local toughs to make trouble. Luke and Bat were honest dealers and expert gunmen. With those two on duty the hoodlums would have to behave.

Bat earned four dollars an hour as a dealer. Most

Bat and some Dodge City friends posed for this picture in 1883. Each man was either a gunman, lawman, or gambler—and some were all three. Standing (left to right): Bill Harris, Luke Short, Bat, and W. F. Petillon. Seated (left to right): Charlie Bassett, Wyatt Earp, Frank McLain, and Neal Brown.

workers did not earn that much in a day! But dealing cards was a risky way to make a living. Losers often blamed the dealer for their bad luck. If they thought the dealer was cheating, they sometimes shot first and asked questions later.

Tombstone soon learned that Wyatt had picked his dealers well. The lesson was driven home after Charlie Storms argued with Luke over a card game. Bat broke up the fight and sent the gambler to his hotel. He warned Storms that tiny Luke Short was tougher than he looked.

Luke was standing outside the saloon when Storms came back. The gambler pulled a pistol, but Luke was faster. He shot Storms through the heart. After that no one challenged the dealers at the Oriental.

As marshal, Wyatt found other uses for Bat's talents. In March he asked Bat to join a posse, along with Morgan and Virgil Earp. Bandits trying to rob a stagecoach had killed two men. Bob Paul, who had ridden shotgun on the stage, named two of the killers. Three days and 150 miles later the posse caught one of the killers. Luther King confessed and gave Wyatt the names of his friends. All were members of the Clanton gang.

The posse pushed on over rocky hills and across scorching desert. The killers' friends gave them fresh horses, but the posse had to make do with tired mounts. The lawmen also ran short of food and water. Bat's hard-ridden horse dropped dead under him. He caught a ride back to Tombstone in a wagon. Wyatt kept going, but he never did catch the killers. He was even more upset when the local sheriff let King go free.

A bloody feud was building between the Earps and the Clantons. Seven months later the two sides met in the famous shootout at the O.K. Corral. Bat was not in Tombstone that day. In April 1881 he had received a telegram from Dodge City. His brother Jim needed help.

Jim Masterson, younger brother of Ed and Bat, was the family's third lawman. The brothers did not always get along. When Jim was in trouble, however, Bat left Tombstone to rush to his rescue.

5

YOU CAN'T WIN 'EM ALL

The telegram that sent Bat to Dodge City was short. "Come at once," it said. "Updegraff and Peacock are going to kill Jim."

When Bat reached Dodge he did not know if Jim was still alive. He did know that a new mayor had fired Jim from his job as town marshal. After that Jim had bought a half share in the Lady Gay saloon. He and his partner, A. J. Peacock, soon began to argue. One problem was that Peacock would not fire a crooked bartender named Al Updegraff. Updegraff, it turned out, was Peacock's brother-in-law. The two men were now planning to kill Jim.

Bat jumped off the train as it coasted into the station. The first men he saw were Peacock and Updegraff. Bat called out, saying he wanted to talk. But the two men ducked behind the jail and opened fire. Bat took cover and shot back.

The shooting brought more men into the battle. Peacock's friends sniped at Bat in his hiding place, while Bat's friends rushed to his defense. Bullets smashed windows and sent townsfolk ducking for cover. After about ten minutes the shooting stopped. Updegraff was lying on the ground, a bullet through his lung. The mayor rushed up and arrested Bat.

Bat was taken to police court. Because Peacock had fired the first shot, a judge went easy on him. Bat

Ham Bell's saloon had George Masterson, youngest of the Masterson brothers, tending bar. When he was not on duty, Bat sometimes played cards here. Gambling tables line the walls of the long, ornate barroom.

pleaded guilty to firing his pistol on a city street and was fined eight dollars. After Jim sold his share in the Lady Gay, the two brothers left town.

Bat and Jim headed west and settled in Trinidad, Colorado. The wide-open town was making good money from cattle and mining. Bat was soon put in charge of the gambling games in one of the town's saloons. Jim took a job with the town police force.

In April 1882 Bat was asked to serve as city marshal. By now his fame had spread across the West. No one dared take him on in a gunfight. Men whispered that he had killed at least 22 men. His pistol, they said, had that many notches in the handle. Bat enjoyed stories like that. Later he bought a used Colt and cut notches in the handle. Then he gave the pistol to a gun collector as a joke.

In May Bat welcomed Wyatt Earp to town. Wyatt and Doc Holliday had left Tombstone after killing the men who murdered Morgan Earp. Now Arizona officials wanted Colorado's police to send Doc back to stand trial. Bat went to Denver and told the governor that Doc could not get a fair trial in Tombstone. The governor agreed and let Doc stay. The gambling dentist died in Colorado five years later of a lung disease.

Life was not always smooth for Bat. That fall a drunk gave him some of his own medicine. The man hit Bat with a cane when the lawman tried to arrest him. Soon after that Bat lost a diamond ring in a street scuffle.

Through all of this he kept on running his gambling games. The voters did not think that was right. In April 1883 they voted Bat out of office.

From Trinidad, Bat moved to Denver. The city became his base, but he made trips throughout the West. Always fond of women, he was now living with a blonde actress named Emma Walters. Emma had been part of Bat's life since he first moved to Trinidad. After they married in 1891 the couple stayed together for 30 years. They never had any children.

Bat's gunfighting days were over, but he still carried his pistols. The guns came in handy one day in Fort Worth, Texas. Bat was visiting his old friend Luke Short at Luke's White Elephant saloon. While he was there Luke killed a gunman in a fair fight. That night Bat heard that a lynch mob was forming. He talked the sheriff into letting him stay with Luke. The mob broke up when it heard the news. No one wanted to face Bat Masterson. Luke was later cleared of all charges.

Back in Denver, Bat bought the Palace Theater and gambling hall. With its crystal fixtures and 60-foot mirror, it was a splendid place. Bat booked the acts for the theater, which held 750 people. He also found time for another interest: boxing.

Bat knew prizefighting, but he often backed losers. He was in Jake Kilrain's corner when Jake lost to John L. Sullivan in 75 bloody rounds. In those days three-minute rounds did not exist. Bareknuckle boxers fought

In 1888, Bat used his gambling winnings to buy the Palace Theater in Denver. The Palace was a saloon, gambling hall, and theater all in one. Owning a fine place like the Palace made Bat one of Denver's most respected citizens.

until one of them was knocked down. Thirty seconds later a new round began. The fight did not end until one boxer could not answer the bell.

In 1896 Bat helped stage a fight between Bob Fitzsimmons and Peter Maher. The fight was to take place in El Paso. But Texas law did not permit prizefighting. Judge Roy Bean then invited the fight crowd to move to Langtry, Texas. That seemed to make sense, because Judge Bean "owned" Langtry. However, the fans found Texas Rangers waiting at Langtry to stop the fight. Thinking quickly Judge Bean told the crowd to wade across the Rio Grande River. Once they were in Mexico, Bat was free to collect $20 from each fan. The high-priced tickets paid for only one round of boxing. Fitzsimmons won by a quick knockout.

In May 1902 Bat's time in Denver came to a sudden end. As he was walking into his local polling place, a woman challenged his right to vote. She had guessed he was about to vote against the women running for the school board. Bat, who was a legal voter, refused to back down. Without warning the woman struck him with her umbrella. Bat turned and left the polling place. He was angry, but hitting women was not in his line.

Depressed by the incident Bat went on a drinking binge. As usual he was carrying a Colt .45—and he was in an ugly mood. The Denver police chief did not want anyone to get hurt. He sent for Jim Marshall, a tough lawman and Bat's good friend. The chief hoped that Marshall could disarm Bat without a gunfight.

Marshall slipped in by a side door and held his gun against Bat's back. In a quiet voice he urged his friend to leave town. Bat sobered up quickly. He did not try to draw on Marshall. Instead, he and Emma left Denver on the four o'clock train. Bat now knew that times were changing. The West no longer welcomed gamblers and gunmen.

6

A NEW LIFE IN THE EAST

Emma and Bat arrived in New York City in the spring of 1902. The former lawman was now almost 50. His hair was graying and he had shaved off his mustache. He had also put on weight. Unlike the early days he preferred prizefights to gunfights. The old fires had not burned out, however. When he was wronged Bat's blue-gray eyes still turned hard with anger.

Bat's first days in the big city gave him reason to be angry. A "mush-headed cop" arrested him. The charges grew out of the train trip to New York. A church elder said Bat and three gamblers had cheated him out of $17,000. Bat was outraged. He prized his standing as an "honest" gambler.

Bat said that he had not even played in the card game. Friends rushed to put up his $500 bail. By that time the church elder was having second thoughts. He

failed to appear in court to press charges. With no wit-
ness on hand the judge dismissed the case. Bat did pay
a $10 fine for carrying a concealed weapon.

Bat's old friends were shocked when they read about
his arrest. William Pinkerton, the great detective, came
to his defense. Pinkerton was quoted as saying that Bat
Masterson "is absolutely honest." For their part New
Yorkers welcomed the Mastersons. The stories about

*Hot Springs, Arkansas was one of Bat's favorite gambling spots. On a
1912 visit, Bat (right) posed with Sydney Burns (left) and William
Pinkerton (center). Pinkerton was head of the famous Pinkerton Detective
Agency. In a city suit and without his moustache, Bat no longer
looked like a gunslinger.*

Adobe Walls and Dodge City were revived. By now Bat was said to have killed 28 men.

After the first shock wore off, Bat liked New York. He enjoyed the bright lights and the active sporting scene. He was soon promoting and refereeing prize-fights. During the racing season he spent relaxed days at the track. Bat knew how to judge horses, and he always placed a few bets.

In 1903 William Lewis of the *Morning Telegraph* hired Bat to write for his daily newspaper. Years earlier Lewis had heard Bat spin tales of frontier life. He also knew that his friend had worked hard to improve his writing.

Early prize fights, as in this photo, were fought in front of huge crowds. Bat promoted some of these matches and refereed others. Many of his newpaper columns were about boxers and the people who ran the sport.

The breezy *Telegraph* was perfect for Bat. The newsroom was a free and easy place. After their work was done the reporters played poker. The editors let Bat write what he wanted to write. As a result he added strong opinions to his stories. Once, in 1906, he went too far in reporting a murder case. When the jury found a defendant guilty, Bat disagreed. He used phrases such as "lynch law" and "mob rule" in his story. The judge in the case said that Bat had gone too far. He fined the newsman $50.

The newspaper soon rewarded Bat by giving him his own column. "Masterson's Views on Timely Topics" ran three days a week. Bat mostly wrote about boxing, but he found time to comment on larger matters, too. He did not pull his punches. Of New York he wrote, "This is the biggest boob town in America." The ban on the sale of liquor upset him. "Personal liberty," he wrote, "has become a ghastly joke in this country."

In 1904 Bat was settled enough to turn down a job offer from President Theodore Roosevelt. The President wanted his old friend to take the post of U.S. Marshal of Oklahoma. Bat wisely wrote, "It wouldn't do. . . . Some kid who was born after I took off my guns would get drunk and look me over. The longer he looked the less he'd be able to see where my reputation came from. . . . In the end he'd crawl around to a gunplay and I'd have to send him over the jump. . . . I've got finally out of that zone of fire and I hope never to go back to it."

Bat never hid his opinions when he wrote for the Morning Telegraph. *Here, a cartoonist pokes fun at Bat warning New York (symbolized by a Knickerbocker, or old Dutch New Yorker) to behave itself.*

"Bat"—"Now, Knick, you be good!"

Bat's friendship with the President dated back to the 1880s. The two men had met in the Dakotas. Although he was raised in the East Roosevelt loved the Wild West and its people. As a young man he once headed a posse that captured some horse thieves. After turning down one lawman's job, Bat did accept another closer to home. Roosevelt made him a deputy U.S. marshal for the southern district of New York. The post was part-time, so Bat could still write for the *Telegraph.*

Roosevelt often invited Bat to the White House. The two men swapped adventure yarns. Bat also gave advice when the President asked for it. Roosevelt loved sports, and Bat introduced him to leading sports figures. Unlike some men Bat never used his friendship with the President for his own gain.

Only once did Bat fail the President. In 1909 Roosevelt invited him to a formal party for the heads of the armed forces. Bat was sure he would be out of place. As an excuse he said he did not have the proper dress clothes. A friend offered to lend Bat the outfit he needed. For once the old lawman's courage failed him. Bat sent a telegram to the friend. It read, "I ain't going to attend any reception. Am heading east. Bat Masterson."

The friendship lasted after Roosevelt left office. Bat

Bat and Emma Masterson gave these portraits to Billy Thompson of Denver in September 1921. A month later, the old lawman was dead. Friends said that Bat, at 67, had become a "gentle old fellow, mellow and good-natured." The gentle and loving Emma may have helped to make him so.

was an advisor when Roosevelt failed to regain the White House in 1912. Then came World War I. Roosevelt offered to raise a division of "outdoor men" to fight in France. Bat wrote to give advice on how Roosevelt should lead the division. The plan died after President Wilson turned it down. Roosevelt died in 1919, leaving Bat to mourn the death of a true friend.

Bat was aging, but he did not slow down. He made one last trip out West. The changes surprised him. He wrote, "The idea that the plains . . . could ever be made fertile was something I never dreamed of."

Back in New York he spent his nights in cafes and bars. He ate thick steaks and talked about the old days. He also liked to watch western films. Western star William S. Hart offered him a part in a film. Bat said he would think about it.

That was October 1921. Two weeks later Bat went to his office to write his column. He had a bad cold and was not feeling well. As usual he wrote about boxers and boxing. Then, as he laid down his pen, his heart stopped beating. He was dead when an assistant looked in a few minutes later.

7

THE LEGEND OF BAT MASTERSON

Bat Masterson was a real gunslinger. He was not invented by hack writers of dime novels. His life contained the stuff from which legends—and films—are made. Bat fought Indians, hunted buffalo, and tamed wild frontier towns. Both friends and foes admired his cool courage and sense of fair play.

Like Wyatt Earp, Bat knew when to hand in his lawman's badge. Somewhere down the trail, he said, was a young gunman waiting to kill him. He could see that the West was changing. In his lifetime the buffalo were nearly wiped out. Indians were confined to their reservations. Shipments by rail replaced the old cattle drives. And the silver mines closed down.

In middle age Bat hung up his guns and became a writer. He found new interests in sports and business. With Emma's help he made a success of his marriage.

After moving to New York he did not waste time yearning for the open plains. He said a weekend in the country would bore him.

Bat was often angry, and perhaps he drank too much. But he was always loyal to his friends. When he died it was "with his boots on," slumped over his desk. That was very likely the way he wanted to go.

The great lawman was buried in New York, far from Dodge City's Boot Hill. The nation was saddened by his death. Letters and telegrams poured in from people great and small. Bat would have enjoyed all of them. Perhaps the truest and simplest tribute came from the *Telegraph*. "William Barclay Masterson," his editor wrote, "was one of the . . . squarest [most honest] men that ever lived."

Bat Masterson died "with his boots on" after a long and colorful career as a lawman, gambler, fight promoter, and newsman. To the American public, Bat represented the untamed spirit of the West.

GLOSSARY

cavalry—Troops trained to fight from horseback.

church elder—A high official of the Mormon Church.

column—A newspaper feature that appears regularly, often under the name of a popular writer.

deputy—A lawman who assists a sheriff or marshal.

dime novels—Low-cost books and magazines that printed popular fiction during the late 1800s.

frontier—A region just being opened to settlers. Life on the frontier was often hard and dangerous.

gatling gun—An early form of the machine gun.

gunslingers—Outlaws and lawmen of the Old West who settled arguments with their pistols.

honky-tonk—A cheap, noisy bar or dance hall.

hoodlums—Tough, destructive men who do not hesitate to break the law.

legend—A story that many people believe, but which is often untrue in whole or in part.

lynch mob—An out-of-control crowd that wants to hang someone, often for a crime the mob's victim did not commit.

posse—A group of citizens who join with lawmen to aid in the capture of outlaws.

railhead—The farthest point to which a railroad's tracks have been laid.

reservation—Land set aside by the government for an Indian tribe to live on.

roundhouse—A circular building where railway locomotives are serviced and repaired.

scout—Someone who goes out ahead of the main body of troops to study the enemy's positions.

MORE GOOD READING ABOUT BAT MASTERSON

Breihan, Carl. "Bat Masterson," in *Great Gunfighters of the West*. San Antonio, Texas: Naylor Company, 1962. pp. 88 –105.

DeArment, Robert. *Bat Masterson: The Man and the Legend*. Norman, Okla.: University of Oklahoma Press, 1979.

Horan, James. "Bat Masterson," in *The Authentic Wild West: The Lawmen*. New York: Crown Publishers, 1980. pp. 21–74.

Lyon, Peter. "Wyatt Earp and Bat Masterson," in *The Wild, Wild West*. New York: Funk & Wagnalls, 1969. pp. 95 –116.

O'Conner, Richard. *Bat Masterson*. New York: Doubleday, 1957.

Rosa, Joseph. *The Gunfighter; Man or Myth?* Norman, Okla.: University of Oklahoma Press, 1969.

INDEX